Legal & Disclaimer

The information contained in this book and its contents is not designed to replace or take the place of any form of medical or professional advice; and is not meant to replace the need for independent medical, financial, legal or other professional advice or services, as may be required. The content and information in this book have been provided for educational and entertainment purposes only.

The content and information contained in this book have been compiled from sources deemed reliable, and it is accurate to the best of the Author's knowledge, information, and belief. However, the Author cannot guarantee its accuracy and validity and cannot be held liable for any errors and/or omissions. Further, changes are periodically made to this book as and when needed. Where appropriate and/or necessary, you must consult a professional (including but not limited to your doctor, attorney, financial advisor or such other professional advisor) before using any of the suggested remedies, techniques, or information in this book.

Upon using the contents and information contained in this book, you agree to hold harmless the Author from and against any damages, costs, and expenses, including any legal fees potentially resulting from the application of any of the information provided by this book. This disclaimer applies to any loss, damages or injury caused by the use and application, whether directly or indirectly, of any advice or information presented, whether for breach of contract, tort, negligence, personal injury, criminal intent, or under any other cause of action.

You agree to accept all risks of using the information presented inside this book.

You agree that by continuing to read this book, where appropriate and/or necessary, you shall consult a professional (including but not limited to your doctor, attorney, or financial advisor or such other advisor as needed) before using any of the suggested remedies, techniques, or information in this book.

e-Business Blueprint:

Your Pass to Financial Freedom

Table of Contents

Introduction

With an economic whiplash that hits the majority of the countries today; more people are joining ranks in achieving economic progress through the internet. The internet world had become an American Dream while others look at it as the other side of the world with the greener pasture.

Many had indeed taken their chance in starting an online business, yet not all are ready to face all the challenges and the complexities of surviving in the internet business arena.

However, for those who were lucky enough to survive, they lived to testify to the kind of life online business offers.

This eBook, "e-Business Blueprint: Your Pass to Financial Freedom" aims to provide beginners with a guide on setting up an online business and guiding you through the simple steps to achieve success.

With proper knowledge and determination, success on any online business can be achievable and in fact, rewarding. It's just a matter of planning and driving your towards a goal that can really make your dream comes true.

CHAPTER 1: Reasons for Getting Into an Online Business

People got different reasons for going into online business. But most often, online business is for people who got tired of working 8-5 or 9-6 every day. Rushing each morning for a gulp of coffee before fighting his way through traffic and hoping he could be earlier than usual!

As you realized that you are getting tired of working for someone else and you want to become your own boss, you start thinking of the possibility to make it big in the internet business. Hoping, you are right, and then the best way to set up a business with a greater chance to make it to success is to start now!

Here are just a few of the many reasons why you have to start with your internet business.

Goodbye to Traffic and Early Morning Rush

With an internet business, you don't need to rush up too early that you need to skip eating breakfast just so you can arrive in time for work. But when you are living in an overcrowded metropolis where you had to go through jam-packed traffic, stress and anxiety can be a daily part of your routine!

Online business can help you save a lot of money by not traveling every day. Count the savings you can have when you don't need to go out for work. You can likewise save your time and convert the time spent for daily trips into more productive inputs.

No Need Putting Up with a Toxic Boss

Most often people got fed up and want to get out of their work because they have a toxic person for a boss. Most often, bosses thought that their employees are there to please them all the time. This often happens when you are working in a sole proprietorship type of business or a one-man organization. Most often than not, you feed to your boss whims and schemes rather than get productive in your tasks. In the end, you feel thoroughly burnt out and find a quick way to change job.

Working at your own Pace and Time

When you are running an online business, you can be your own boss. You can work at a chosen time and place. You can even have more time to yourself and to your family. However, this can have its own drawback. So before you get out of your work, be sure your finances or the lack of will not cripple you. Proper timing is needed so your family will not suffer from your decision.

When you are free to decide for yourself whether you are going to work or not, be sure you manage your time effectively and efficiently. When you're alone to manage your time and no one is around to put pressure on you, you don't give yourself a reason to procrastinate. You need to learn to balance everything even without someone to answer to. Remember that every minute wasted is an opportunity lost in online business.

Unlimited Income Potential

Working on a regular career means putting up a cap on how much you can earn. But with online business, your ability to earn depends on how much time you want to put into your business. You can earn as much or as little as you want. The market for online business is too vast. You just learn to tap its unlimited resources and you go as far as you can.

You can target people around the world as the global market is getting bigger and bigger and more people are learning how to access the internet every day. You can work as much or as little as you choose. The marketplace for internet businesses is worldwide.

According to the later report of the Statistics portal, the number of internet users had risen up to 3.17 billion this year from 2.94 of the previous year. Isn't that market large enough to dip your toes into?

Minimal Expenses for an Office

Since you are working from the comfort of your home, you don't need to rent an office space. You will again be saving a lot on your administrative expenses compared if you are running a conventional type of business.

In setting up your business, all you need to have is your laptop or PC and low-cost hardware and software which you can even get for free online if you're just diligent enough to browse through your internet.

Bigger Chance to Achieve more for Less Work

An online business allows you to work fewer hours and achieve more. There are some business models that can be fully automated. You just have to set them up and (lo!), they can run on their own and earns you a passive income. This automation process now is widely used in the internet market. If you can't run your business on 100% automation, you can at least have it automated at 50% or more, so you can have more time for additional business to carry on.

What makes an online business unique than conventional ones is you can operate multiple businesses single-handedly. To simplify, you are operating a business that is almost next to impossible – Less capital, less time, and less effort for unlimited income streams potentials.

Common Problems you will Encounter at the Start of your Online Business

Starting your online business can be both rewarding and stimulating. However, you are sure to encounter a few problems that new entrepreneurs usually encounter. To steer clear of these issues, you must be aware of them and avoid them as they come along.

Tempting Opportunities and Resources

As you start hanging on the internet, you will be meeting a lot of opportunities along with remarkable resources to promising you great support in your online business. These products, usually software or a business opportunity, may be as great as their vendor advertise them. Nonetheless, if you jump from one opportunity to another, you will be losing your focus on your core business. It is, therefore, important that you start an online business with only what you absolutely need and have it run smoothly before getting into another. The same works with your software or any other tool.

Neglecting New Opportunities

Basically, this is the exact opposite of grabbing every opportunity that comes along. If you refuse to examine or look at any new opportunity sent your way because you have your focus set up trying to achieve a goal with a method that simply don't work, avoid overlooking the warning signs that tell you that you need to move on or move in another direction.

Doing Everything by Yourself

When you think it's better to keep all the profit, you keep trying to do everything so you can keep the money to yourself. Saving is always good for your business, but as your business develops, it will become impossible for you to embrace all the tasks. This is the time when you need to develop some way to ease up your workload. An example of these if subscribing for an auto responder that will take care of your mailing activities. Instead of manually sending letters, answering queries, the auto-responder allows you to maintain and develop relationships with your customer base and up-sell or cross-sell your products and services.

Having Too Many Choices

Affiliate marketing is a good start for an online business for you can earn as soon as someone buys from your inks. This is the reason why it is so popular with many people.

Affiliate marketing method has many positive aspects but there are too many choices that it is confusing to know which to promote. Before you jump into marketing a new software by way of an affiliate program, check how much commission you can earn from it, how you can get paid, and know if there is some support you can get from the owner. It is also important to know if the product actually sells before promoting it.

The Internet is Bigger than What you Think

Having an online business doesn't mean that people will naturally visit your website and buy things that you offer. The internet is such an enormous marketplace that you need to know how to get prospective customers to visit your visit so you can have the chance to convert these visits into sales. Meaning, you need to learn how to generate website traffic by utilizing both free and paid traffic generators.

No Support from Family and Friend

Sometimes, we presume that our family and friends will be our loyal customer. Sad to say, in most cases, it doesn't usually happen especially during the start of your business. There are even cases when they will discourage you from doing online business. Though these people mean well, don't get easily swayed and let your goals and efforts get destructed. If you have set your goal and created a business plan to back it up, you have every opportunity to get successful.

Regardless of whom you are, your age, gender, technical skills, educational background, you can always start your own internet business. You can always harness whatever skill you have through various learning platforms and resources provided on the internet for a certain fee or for free.

CHAPTER 2: Turning Your Passion into Profit

If there's one thing that really great with online business, it is the fact that it can revolve around your passion, skills and interest. Being new in the internet arena, you will be overwhelmed by the enormity of choice you can have in selecting what kind of business you can get into. As soon as you start connecting, making known to others that you are interested in getting into the business, hundreds of websites are just too eager to offer you choices. A new business is born almost every minute and the majority of them offer great potentials.

However, turning a hobby into a business is more likely to succeed because you are passionate and highly motivated to do things that interest you. How would you feel if you are being paid for something you want to do? Of course, one thing is sure here – you spend more time and effort doing something that you love to do. The same thing works in business. If you love doing the kind of business you have, then you enjoy every moment doing something for your business.

Some people fail in online business even before they can have their take off because they are not enjoying what they are doing. That's what makes it a difficult task. But if you are enjoying doing it, nothing is too heavy for you and before you realize it, you are done with it and have done it real good!

Your dream can turn into a frightening nightmare of responsibilities if you have not readied yourself before taking your course. So before you start getting any form of online business, try to take a reality test. Know if your hobby can realistically get you somewhere.

Choose the Hobby to Start With

You may have a lot of hobbies. This is good for you as it means, you have a lot of skills to go along with them. Nonetheless, you may get too overwhelmed. Choose one of your great preferences when you're still at the start of your business. You may choose the one where you excel best. Let's say you are good in selling anything. Then you know you can use that ability in a marketing business.

Do Some Research on your Hobby

As a business entrepreneur, you need to determine if there is an existing market for your particular line of interest, hobby or passion. It's not enough to go into business just because you love doing that particular task. Hence, if you love writing and you have that passion for writing anything, you have to know what others are doing to market this kind of skill.

Know the specific demand

By knowing what's trending, you will know what writing tasks are in demand in the market. If your passion is writing poems, definitely you know if there is a market for your poems. Maybe you can start your research with greeting cards publishers. You will also be able to find in your research available guidelines that you need to follow when you market your skill.

If you are good in marketing, this can be a good start for you. Marketing is highly in demand on the internet. You can start and join an affiliation marketing program and you can earn as soon as you are able to make a sale. Affiliation marketing programs are a potential source of income for beginners and don't need much of your time. You can even have them on the sideline.

Follow it up by a Market Research

When you are in marketing, you will realize that there is much competition out there. However, an in-depth market analysis of your products can help a lot to get you great head start. You may be new in the internet world, but marketing principles are still the same. The more knowledgeable you are with the product you are selling, the more edge you have against your competitors.

Having a marketing research should provide you data on the specifications of the product you are selling. People are very particular about the quality of the product and since there are more products of that kind available in the market, you must not disregard the quality.

Even if your service is excellent if the product is not good enough to provide customers satisfaction, you will not get a higher conversion rate for the product.

As you do your marketing research, gather information relative to the following.

Product

Determine the product standing or the company behind the product you intend to market. You can have an insight on the product by reading reviews and testimonies. Just make a search on the specific product and the search engine is quick enough to provide you with data relevant to your search.

Products are usually introduced or are being market by way of information campaign. You can read articles about them and how they perform to meet customer satisfaction but do not neglect to read comments of people you can find at the bottom of the articles. They will help you gauge the quality and performance of the product.

You will also read reviews provided by consumers and people who are in the same trade as you. Learn from them. One thing that is great with the internet is the fact that it allows you to directly interact with anyone even if you do not know them. When you can find articles regarding the product, interact with the publisher or other people who provide comments and opinions on the product.

Besides gaining enough knowledge on the product through the interaction, this can also be a great way to start a connection with these people. Contacts and connections are important in your marketing business or whatever business you will put up in the future.

Demand

As you browse on the internet for the specific product, and the search engine provides you with a glimpse on the relevant keywords, you will know if there is a specific market for the product. The existence of a market implies that there is an existing demand.

When there is great competition in a target market, it is because the product is highly in demand.

As an entrepreneur, choose a product with a big demand. You can also choose a product with average demand and lesser competition. When you can't compete with big and old-time marketers, and then opt for a possible product that is less competitive but can bring you great results. After all, a good marketer can sell even a bad spoiled tomato. Just don't forget nor bypass your principles of marketing. The word of mouth in marketing can still make or break a marketer.

Competition

Competition is like a school of fishes in an open sea. Just like you and me. There are too many people who are willing to take their shot at the abundance of the internet ocean and who would not? Given all the potentials and opportunities this world can offer, no one can fail to see what they are missing.

The competition is what creates you above the rest. There may be too many of you marketing the same piece of product, offering the same price and from the same source. But if you truly know what you are doing, having done some adequate research on the product and market before diving into the ocean of opportunities, then there's no reason for you to success.

Those who lose are those who procrastinates, cowards, and lazy. Others may not be that smart but their passion and motivation to learn and surpass every hindrance in their business are what makes them rise above others. You are one of these men if you have the quality of a hardworking ant, the meekness of the lamb, but the shrewdness of a serpent.

Conducting SWOT Analysis

If you are not aware of what a SWOT analysis is, it is an acronym for S strengths, W – weaknesses, O – opportunities, and T – threats.

SWOT analysis is an essential tool in making situational analysis before getting into a business venture. This is assessing your business strengths, weaknesses, market opportunities, and threats through a very simple, logical process that can offer powerful insight into the potential and critical issues affecting your target market venture.

The SWOT analysis starts by listing an inventory of strengths and weakness. Note that this process forces you to focus on every aspect related to your business which you can't possibly do once you leap directly into business without any prior planning.

Identify the external threats and opportunities that can affect the business operation based on the market and overall business environment. You need not go over every detail but take the bullet points to begin with. Simply list down the factors which you think are significant to each of these four specific areas. You will still be reviewing everything that you have listed here as you work through with your business plan.

It is the primary purpose of your SWOT analysis to be able to determine and designate each individual factor, whether they have positive or negative significance, to each of the four groups. This process allows you to have an objective view of your business. This will be useful in confirming your goal and marketing strategy.

Strengths

Under this category, determine the positive attributes, both tangible and intangible relative to your business. Are they controllable? What are your resources and where do you excel most? What are your advantages over your competitors?

Strengths can include tangible resources available like capital, equipment (Computers, software, hardware, devices, etc.), existing contacts and social media memberships, and other online resources you can use in your business. Your strengths characterize the positive aspects internal to your business and likewise add value or offer you a competitive edge.

Weaknesses

Weaknesses are those factors that you can manipulate but can detract you from your ability to obtain or maintain an edge in a market competition. Which areas can you have greater potential for improvement.

Weaknesses can represent your lack of knowledge, lack of access or skills limited resources, technology or poor business location. These factors can be controllable but for a variety of reasons, need to be enhanced for the accomplishment of your marketing objectives.

Weaknesses place you at a competitive disadvantage while it represents the negative factors inherent in your business, detracting you from the value that you offer. Don't minimize or neglect existing weakness while making your SWOT analysis as factors in this category are greatly needed to enhance the best competition. Hence, the more accurate in determining and dealing with your weakness and limitations, the more significant the SWOT in your overall analysis or assessment.

Opportunities

Opportunities represent factors outside your business which poses as attractive potentials that give your business reasons to continue and prosper. Identify existing opportunities. Identify opportunities that are present in your market or in the environment which can be useful to you. Opportunities can be the result of market development, change in lifestyles, positive market forecast about your business, resolution of problems relevant to current situations, or the potential to offer greater worth that will create opportunities for your business.

- Opportunities include:
- Local and Global events
- Potential new uses of products and/or services
- Changes in technology and markets
- Changes in government policy or regulations/legislation in your favor
- Use of marketing or promotional techniques to boost the business
- Social factors such as population fluctuations, lifestyle, changes, etc.

The potentials somehow reflect the potential you can realize when implementing your marketing strategies. Expected opportunities that are inherent to the business and within your control can be classified as your strength.

Threats

What can intimidate your business operation? Threats are those factors which are not within your control. They can put your marketing strategy and the whole business at risk. Since they are external, you can't manipulate them. However, having contingency plans can help address them once they occur and threaten your business.

Factors that threaten your business are challenges created by an unfavorable market movements or growth that may lead to deteriorating revenues or profits. A major threat can be in the form of an existing or potential competition. Other threats are intolerable price hike mandated by suppliers, economic crisis, devastating media and press coverage, government regulation that can affect your sales, a change in consumer behavior causing your sales to decrease or an introduction of a new technology or innovation that can make your offers of products or services too obsolete.

Be sure to list down all factors that can prove to be a menace to your marketing efforts and lay all your nightmares on the table. They can be speculative but having them as mechanisms of your SWOT analysis can do a lot to help.

Classify these threats according to their seriousness and probability of occurrence. The more you are likely to identify potential threats, the easier for you to make proactive plans in response to these threats. You will need your SWOT analysis once you are face to face with them in your future operation.

The implication

The real value of the SWOT analysis is in bringing all the information with regard to the four factors together in assessing the most promising opportunities, and the most crucial issues.

The internal factors – strengths and weaknesses – in comparison to external factors – opportunities and strengths – can offer additional insights into the current standing and potential of the business. Let's say, how you could make use of your strengths to maneuver opportunities to your maximum advantage. Can you reverse the effects that threats can cause you if they turn out to be a reality?

Formulate your Business Plan

Formulating your business plan based on your conducted research and analysis is actually putting it down in writing. This will serve as your technical guide in the operation of your business.

Try some Market Testing

Once you had established what kind of products or services to offer, try to have a test of that product in the market. If you are a writer you would be launching soon a new book, try to give away some samples to some friends or loyal followers and have them post some reviews.

Through this, you will be able to get their reaction to the product before you have it fully launched in the market. If there are some negative reviews on it, try making some changes or improvements before finally launching the product.

Finding a Unique Selling Proposition

Because competition is something you must reckon with on the internet if you intend to achieve success, then you must find ways to position yourself in the lead. This means that you have to do more than just selling.

Just because you love to write, it does not necessarily mean that people will buy anything that you write. You had to establish yourself in the mind of the readers that you have previously sold bestseller books before you can do that.

A unique selling proposition is often overlooked but it is a very important element of creating a business that customers love. It defines your business unique position in the marketplace and sets you apart from competitors while actively focus your energy on catering to the needs of your specific target group of customers in a specific niche.

Why do you Need to have a Unique Selling Proposition?

In a great wave of competition, consumers usually find it hard to choose the one that is different from others – the one that deserves their trust, time, and money. Making the best selection can be daunting for consumers who don't have the experience to identify what separates one competitor from the rest.

As a good online business entrepreneur, it is your responsibility to help them by making a unique selling proposition that is obvious, different and easy to identify so they can quickly identify what your business has to offer that your competitors don't. In order to be easily remembered in a crowded competition, it helps that your business carries a trait that is worth remembering.

Differentiation is an important strategic and tactical activity. While a superior product and outstanding services are the major components of a growing online business, differentiation use as a competitive advantage can always make you stand out like a sore thumb.

How to Develop a Unique Selling Proposition that Works

The idea of a developing a unique selling proposition is not to work out to be the BEST but to be DIFFERENT. In a vast competition, working out to be the best will not set you apart from the rest. However, working out to be DIFFERENT will surely catch out people's interest.

Changing the rule of the game is the idea here. Competition won't be able to have its claws on you if you change the rule of the game. After all, people are commonly after something that is NEW and UNIQUE. If you can introduce a new game, the better it is for them.

CHAPTER 3: Getting Things Ready – The Business Plan

As soon as you are ready and strongly convinced that you want to put up an online business, you have to start formulating your business plan. The business plan can serve as your guide as you go along the way.

Without a business plan to guide you, you will be engulfed in the vastness of the internet world. Every business needs to have a business plan in order to be successful. It doesn't matter if it is online or a tangible company that is manned with a large manpower.

Before you get yourself into a certain type of business, it is a must that you have enough knowledge of what you're letting yourself into. After all, you won't dare to go somewhere you are in total ignorance. Fear and anxiety arise when you are in the dark and sure enough, you don't want any of these to happen to you.

Formulating a business plan at the start will force you to seek knowledge related to the business you have chosen. The first thing you want to know of course is if you can really earn something out of this online business.

What is a Business Plan?

A business plan is everything about your business, conceptualized and written down to give a more detailed and distinct quality. You need to put down everything in writing so you will remember details and will not get lost along the way. By doing your business plan, you are forced to think objectively about the details that are necessary for the operation of your business.

When you fail to think about the operation of your business no matter how simple it can be, you will soon find it hard to   things that you failed to recognize earlier. There are important details that need to be taken care of in business before actually getting into operations.

Goal Setting

The minute you consider doing a business, you start setting up a goal. It will serve as your driving factor that will motivate you to achieve success. When there is a specific goal set before any competition, every player's focus, action and determination are solely on that goal. Any distraction away from it will lessen your chance to bring home the bacon.

The same method applies to business, focus on it and don't be distracted by anything, not even by your competitors. Your ability to maintain a cool presence regardless of the existing condition is what makes you a perfect entrepreneur. Without a goal to which you can have your focus to is difficult.

Set of objectives

To back up your goal which is long-term in nature, provide a set of objectives which you need to achieve in a shorter term. These objectives aim to guide and assist you on some things that you need to accomplish in a certain period of time in support of the goal you want to achieve.

For instance, when you are still at the initial stage of your business, your objective is set on surviving. However, as the business grows and begins to win a share in the market, the objective is more likely to shift and geared towards expansion and boosting profit.

Now, being newbies to online business, you need to develop a set of goals for your business. The best objectives are set towards following the SMART principle.

- **S – specific**

It needs to be clearly stated and well-defined. An example is "to increase profit".

- **M – measurable**

It must be measurable with the desired outcome that is a number value that can be measured. An example is "to increase profit by at least 10 percent".

- **A – attainable**

Be sure that the objective that you have set is not impossible. When an objective is attainable, then you are driven to work it out in the soonest possible time. But when you know it is impossible, no amount of time, effort, or investment can turn it into a reality.

- **R- realistic**

Given the possible resources like the financial resources available and with your available skill, time, and effort, the target is becoming possible.

- **T – time bound**

The objective that you set is expected to be completed within a specific schedule or within a given period of time. Let's say within a 12-month timeframe.

Smart objectives allow you to assess your performance from time to time and make adjustments for better improvement.

CHAPTER 4: Creating Your Domain – The Workplace

When you are starting your business, you consider your workplace among other things.

Your workplace is actually a representation of who you are, so make sure it represents the good and nice sides of you. It is where you start your business and it where customers expect to find your products. Your workplace showcases everything that one wants to know and see in you.

In the internet world, your domain is your workplace and your showground. When you set up your business, this is where you need to get a fresh start.

If you are serious about online business, then you have to create your domain. A domain is your business address. An example of a domain is yahoo.com for the sake of those who are new to the internet and don't know what a domain is.

Build a Professional Website

Your business as we have stated previously stated can be based on your hobby but having a professional-looking website is important if you want your business to succeed. Being a beginner, you may not realize this, but the appropriate domain is important to your success on the internet.

Having a website that does not look professional will have its bad impact on your business. So if at first, you don't have the capability to create a website that can't reflect the kind of business personality you want to emit, then, have it done by a professional web designer. You need to have a website that can totally knock out every viewer and send them pulling out their credit cards.

Fill your Website with Useful and Relevant Contents

You may come across an internet adage that says, "Content is King." This is because internet users prefer to indulge their viewing time on useful contents that arouse human interest. Hence, the only way to have viewers flocked and stay longer on your website and later purchased some products are through your contents.

Make sure that your contents are relevant to your site. Your niche chooses the kind of contents that should stay there. Search engines like Google, Yahoo, and Bing are very strict with their rules regarding relevant contents.

Websites that fail to follow their rules and regulations regarding this will face penalties even before they know it.

Your Website is your Online Brochure

Use your website as an online brochure for your products and services offered to customers. Since your website will showcase all your products and services, you have to make sure that all pages are easy to navigate and comprehensible. Viewer won't waste their precious time waiting while your site is loading. Same thing that they won't stay long enough if your content is not easy to read and understand.

Tips in Registering your Domain

You have to consider a lot of things in registering your domain name. To guide you on this, here are some valuable tips. Once you have settled on a domain name, it is quite difficult to change it.

A Choice Between Keyword or Business Name

In choosing a name, some people would choose between a keyword or a business name?

There are always pros and cons in having your choices. When your keyword is relevant to your site niche, it will rank better and a viewer is more likely to search for keywords in searching for a product they want to buy or on a certain topic they want to read rather than search for a brand name when they had never heard of it before. Domain names using keywords are great for websites dedicated to a particular theme or subject. However, since a lot of people are after keywords, it could be quite hard to register some keyword choices. Most of the best keywords are most often taken or registered.

Keywords are not also applicable when you intend to sell multiple products or if you wish to enhance your business in the future and keywords will no longer be relevant then.

On the other hand, when you are registering your domain name using your business name, then you are open to selling any products or services you want. You can even make a shift from what you are starting when in the future; you find your plans not working well with your present offers.

Consider Simplicity

No matter what way you choose in your name selection, make sure that it is simple, easy to recognize and remember. Short names are quick to remember than long ones. Domain names that are memorable are also easy to remember. Some prefer unique but short domain names to create interest and leave something in people's memory.

Avoid Numbers

If you use numbers in your domain name, people aren't really trying to figure out if you are using the number in figures or in the word. This makes it hard to remember, so better to stay away from choosing a number name.

Location

If you prefer running a business in a specific geographical location, then try to include the location in your domain name as long as it does not complicate the whole thing.

Trademarks

Be sure that the name you are choosing for your domain is not yet trademarked by someone else. You can be in a lot of trouble if you did not and find out later that it had been trademarked by another.

In addition, here are some final tips.

Keep your domain name easy to spell. Those that are often times misspelled are also hard to remember. Viewers are not willing to spend time trying to remember the correct spelling and would rather search for other sites as well.

Never use hyphenated domain names as they are not easy to remember and may not rank well with search engines.

As much as possible, stick to the .com domain as people often remember this compared to other domain extensions.

Lastly, don't just register the domain name you had chosen but also register a number of variations of the name. This will ensure that others are prevented from registering similar names. Doing it this way won't cost you too much and you can always redirect then so that traffic on those sites will redirect to your main website.

CHAPTER 5: Developing your Brand – The Product

When you are selling something, may it be a product or a service that you offer, branding is important. It can be a name, term, design or symbol, logo or any combination of these elements that identify the products or the services. These elements are unique and distinguished them from other sellers.

When you are on online business, it is important that you brand yourself as the owner of the site or as an authority on the niche aside from the product. Because trust is important in building a relationship with your customer base, it is relatively important that your customers know you and they can interact with you as well. In other words, the more visible you are to the public, the more than you will be able to gain their trust and confidence.

In the internet arena, people are more likely to buy your product at first because of you and not because of the product itself. This is why branding is important as it pulls people towards you.

As you are establishing a name for your website, you are also establishing a name for yourself on the internet. Branding is not only encouraging your target market to choose you over your competitors but it is also getting your prospects see you as the sole provider of the solution to their problem or need.

Visibility is a must if you want to be remembered by. This is why you need to maintain a regular blog to keep in touch with your viewers. Blogging is a good way of talking about your products and service, informing people of how they are useful to them and at the same time, letting your viewers know things about you.

When your viewer can trust you with your ideas and you were able to gain their trust and confidence, you can see that their visits are converted into sales.

A good brand aims to establish the following across the internet:

- Clearly deliver the message you are sending

- Emotionally relate your prospects and potential customers to your products and services
- Confirms your credibility
- Motivates buyers to purchase your products or hire your services.
- Creates customers loyalty

To be effective in branding, you must understand the needs and wants of your customers, both loyal and potential. This is achieved by integrating your brand strategies at every point of public contact. It is imperative that you must think of branding as an expression of who you are as a representation of your business and what you offer.

When consumers begin to identify with you, your brand will live within the hearts and minds. Branding is the totality of their experiences and perceptions, some of which you can influence. As competition for customers intensify day by day, it is important to spend more time investing in researching, building and defining your brand. After all, your brand is your promise to your customers.

The brand is a major component of your marketing communication and one you don't want to be without. Your brand serves as a guide to understanding the purpose of business objectives while it enables you to align a marketing plan with those objectives and fulfill overall business strategy.

A brand's effectiveness does not happen before the purchase; however, it's about the life of the brand and the experience it gives the customers. A good brand must be able to answer the following:

- Did the product or service perform as expected?
- Was the quality as good as promised?
- How was the service experienced?

If you get positive answers to the above questions, then you've got loyal customers.

CHAPTER 6: Building Your Network – The Market

As a beginner in online business, one of your main concerns is building your customer base as it will serve as your market for products and services you are offering. This is a hard task to begin with as people buy only from the business they trust.

To increase your customer base, it is imperative to be constantly visible and stay in contact with potential and existing customers while offering more value to customers. This way, they will likely remain to be loyal. However, you need a 5% increase in customer retention to have 75% increase result in customer value. So the problem lies on how to improve your customer retention by 5 percent.

Here are some ways to bring in more customers in order for you to increase your customer base.

Offer Newsletter Subscription

Offering subscriptions like newsletters is a way of getting regular contact with your customer base. This is also a great way of building your mail list which is the core of every marketing campaign. As a marketer would commonly say, "Money is on the list," inviting your viewers to sign up for a newsletter subscription will do you many good things.

You can easily connect your sign up page to your mailing list and/or responder to make things easy for. An example of this is the Mail chimp which is for free while you are still starting to gather your first 2,000 subscriptions. After that, you will be paying a minimal amount per month to continue with their services.

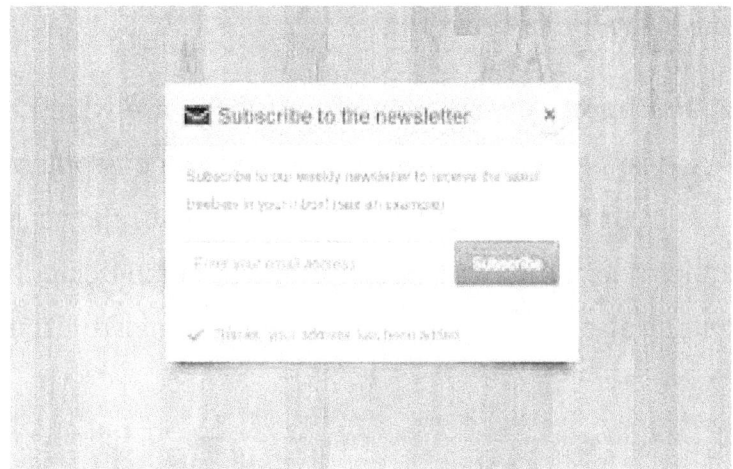

Ask for Customers Opinions

Before a viewer leaves your website, ask them to leave a comment or their opinion either on the product, service or their experience. They are just too happy to have their say on anything. This is one way of interacting with your customer and telling them that you care. While you hear them and see their point of views, you can improve the value of your products and services as well as your customer's value. You may also use short and simple surveys to conduct industry research, customers experience and customer satisfaction.

Maintain Superb Excellent Customer Support and Service

A customer who contacts customer support is someone who truly valued your product and service rather than the one who just turns away without telling you how they feel about the product or service. By giving the kind of service that the customers expect from you or by simply taking an action, you can expect a loyal customer out of this one. And maybe not just one for that kind of customer can always pass a recommendation to others, thus, helping your increase your customer base. A satisfied ad delighted customer can always lead to more sales and recommendations.

Maintain a Fresh Website Content

The fresh and informative content of a website are what draw new visitors to it. From among these visitors, you can have your potential customers so make it a habit of posting fresh content or regularly publishing a blog that reports current business news, hot items and topics relevant to your niche or maybe some ticklers to keep your business alive. Fresh content also allows your website more opportunity to be found in search engines.

Promote in Social Media Networks

Promoting through the social media is the fastest and the easiest way to have your business across the world. An average number of friends that a Facebook user can have are more than two hundred. When you publish a new blog, run a new campaign or launch a new product, the least that you can do is to share it with your friends in social media who in return would share them with others. In lesser time than when you actually promote offline, you can easily reach out to a large number of groups. Just make sure that you deliver useful and interesting content to motivate others to share and re-share them. Isn't this a great way to grow your customer base?

Remember that in social media, you have your own set of friends or contacts, which also have their own set of connections. You can not only reach to your own network but you can, in fact, connect with your friends' own networks and so on. It is an expandable network frame. If you want to reach out to more people, simply add more friends and you can grow them large enough to expand your customer base.

CHAPTER 7: Promoting your Business – Advertising

Everyone knows what a good advertising can do to promote a business-physical or online.

Advertising is an essential tool in marketing. Even if you have the best product and services, you just can't rely alone on the word of mouth or recommendations. It is not enough to keep your online business thrives against the multitudes of competitors.

In today's market, you have to establish an online presence to reach a large customer base and connect with consumers.

Creating Online Presence

Creating a Professional Website

Just as we have previously discussed in other chapters prior to this one, you will need at least one professional website to showcase your product, create your brand and connect with your customer base and potential customers. This is where you are to focus your efforts on improving your business.

Use Local Listing Services

To attract local business, sign up for services like Google Maps or local Yahoo searches that are currently operating like Google, Yahoo or Bing.

Aside from getting you listed on these directories and making your business available for searches, these services also allow you to post photos and graphics, real-time updates and other information like parking tips. They likewise allow customers to post previews of business and to top it all, they are for FREE.

Invest in SEO

As a beginner, you may not easily understand what SEO is all about. SEO is short for Search Engine Optimization. By optimizing your search engine tools and requirements, major search engines will include your webpage on the first few pages of search results.

You may ask why you need to be on any of these first few pages. The answer is simple. When you are a user, you usually start searching for information that you need in the search engine's search bar. You can find this on your browser near the magnifying glass icon. As you search using keywords, the search engine will then find them for you and bring you to the first page of the search result. From there, you may find what you're searching for through browsing different pages. If your page happens to be one of them, only then can your website page be viewed. Since your sales rely on your viewers, you need more viewers to your page. To do this, you need to invest in your SEO as part of your marketing and advertising strategies.

If you are a business owner, even if you happen to be a newcomer in online business, then you probably understand what good advertising can do to your business. As a business entrepreneur, you would like many people to know about your merchandise and services and where to exactly find them. This is applicable to both online and offline business.

Other ways to optimize your website include writing interesting, useful and relevant content, using tags and posting images so people who are using image searches are brought to your website.

Advertise to your customer base

Online advertising is generally costly especially if intended to reach large groups of people. By targeting your advertisement, you will be able to attract the type of traffic you want to your website.

There are online services that display your advertisement to customers in relevant websites and those who make relevant searches. This will likely increase the chances that viewers of your ad will actually click through it. An example of these online services is Google AdWords. There are also other search engines that offer this kind of service. However, you may search for free advertising. There are lots of free websites offering this service including Adboards, Craig's list, Backpages, etc.

Another way to advertise to your customer base is to connect with websites that are not your direct competitors and see if they allow trading website ads. If they allow you to post some ads on their websites, they will also post some of their ads on yours.

Utilize Social Media Networks

Social Media Networks like Twitter, Facebook, LinkedIn and Pinterest have become a necessary tool for doing business. Take time to join on these free social media sites and create interesting profiles or community pages on each of these platforms.

Send Out Press Releases

This can be a great way of getting your ads published on targeted and widely read publications. You can have a press release when you're launching a new product or announcing a sales record to create a good public image for your business.

Connecting with Customers

Writing a Blog

Maintain a blog especially an interesting one and you can draw and keep customers in by way of involving them in your business. It is necessary to post regularly if not daily especially for a beginner like you to hold customers attention.

CHAPTER 8: Managing your Resources

The very basic of all resources that we have is time. Working online may give a leeway of your time but it doesn't mean you can have more time for leisure and recreation. You need more time online that what you really think. Though there's no one to require you to spend more time, the vast opportunities make it possible that you will need more time that you expect.

To be able to manage your time and spend it productively, you need to avail of some resources – tools and apps that you can use to manage your resources – especially time and effort. But what tools are most helpful when you are getting started?

We all know that most often, there are too many details that you need to remember and you can easily get lost in a labyrinth of choices. But you must take the time to provide the most benefit to your business.

Task Management

One problem you are likely to encounter is keeping everything organized. To keep things in proper order, you need to organize your task through a task management system. The internet provides countless solution an again this can be confusing. You will find it hard deciding which is the best. Everything will depend on what you are looking for and how much functionality is required.

Here are some of the management tools you may try and see if they can work great for you.

Asana – This works well with any type of company and has a simple interface. You can work on it alone or with your team. You can also invite others to work on it with some specific task. It is a great way to start using this task manager and you can avail of a free account while learning the use of its features.

Teambox - is another collaborating platform for managing tasks. It allows multiple project workspaces so you can organize tasks between different online products or even completely different companies. Teambox also includes an interactive feature where you can manage other members of your team.

Trello – It's another collaboration tool that comes with a free price tag. Trello organizes your projects into boards and tells you what's being worked on, who's working on something and if anything is still in process. Though it's simple and does not offer many features like in any other project management tools, the interface is more focused on tasks/project than on collaboration works.

Collaboration task can be an effort but online cloud hosting platforms make it much more easily with their file-sharing feature.

Data Storage and File-Sharing

Dropbox – If you want a powerful solution for keeping your files organized and easy sharing with other people, then you must consider using Dropbox. It offers a free plan with limited files for storage. However, you can add more to your storage space by upgrading your account by inviting others to join you on this platform. The interface is simple and easy as you can just drag and drop files to upload into your account. You can even download entire folders of content as .zip containers right from the website. It is indeed great for collaboration efforts.

Social Media Services

If you want to create an online presence especially when branding and promoting your products and services online, you need to register your own accounts in any or all of social networking sites that offer social media services like Facebook, Twitter, LinkedIn, VK, and so on...

Nonetheless, having too many social media sites means too much time and efforts need in managing these sites. To help you in these tasks, here are some tools to lighten your responsibilities.

GrabInBox – An easy way to manage multiple social networks accounts and quickly schedule messages on Facebook and twitter.

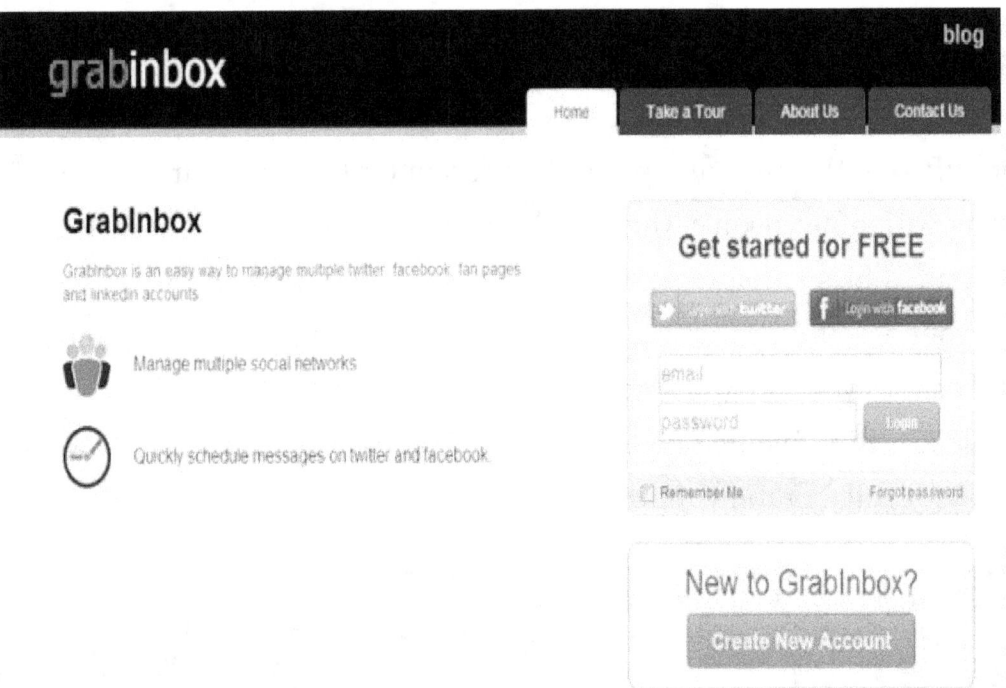

HootSuite – A proven professional solution with a free account. You can easily manage your social profiles from Twitter, GooglePlus, FaceBook, LinkedIn and much more.

UI/UX Testing – These stand for User Interface (UI) and User experience (UE). Bothe deals with the relationship of the product to its users. While User interface deals with the interaction between the user and the product, user experience deals with the sensitivity and reception to the users.

Browser Stack – Unluckily, service is not available for free but it's a great support for browser testing. You can easily create screenshots from any browser and saves you time in squashing bugs if your site is not rendering properly for a certain browser version. It also allows you to run tests on more complicated features like JavaScript or responsive CSS within legacy browsers.

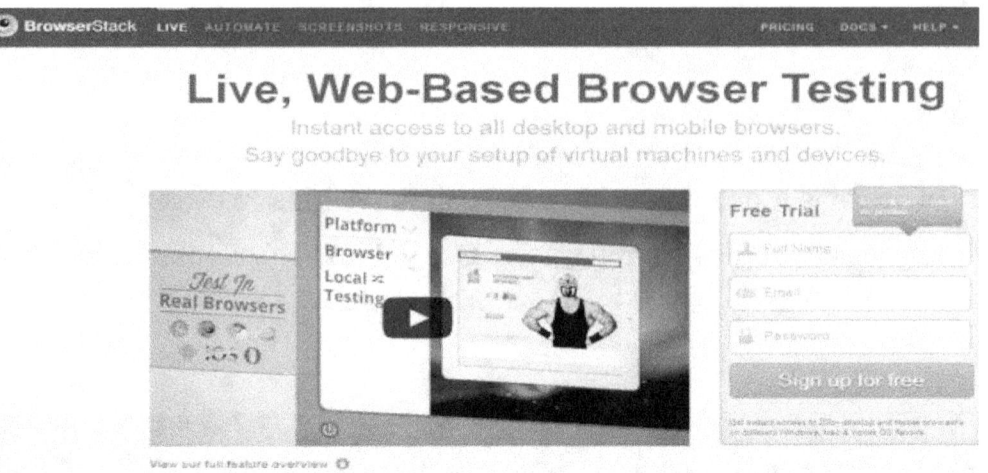

Visual Web Optimizer – Allows you to run A/B split testing on your website and track user analytics to learn from the results. When you are still beginning in your business, you don't really need this and it would be quite hard for you to understand its use. But as you grow and stay long enough, you will learn that optimizing the user experience is crucial for obtaining the best result and delivering the best product to your website for your visitors or viewers.

Support and User Feedback

While your business deals with interaction to customers, it is best to have some support management application available on your website. Even if you are building a web app, it is beneficial for you to have gather feedbacks from your audience as they know what's best for them. With enough testing and feedbacks, you can always improve any projects to be working as efficiently as possible.

Intercom – This app is an online service for handling user support problems. With a typical web-based helpdesk along with customer relationship management tools, Intercom is a perfect system for overseeing your project with clients or customers. Even a free social network can find Intercom useful for managing support questions. A free plan is also available and a great way to use with features and determine if it is indeed beneficial to your project.

UserVoice – can assist you in handling direct feedbacks. With a tiny widget set up on your site, visitors can directly send messages to your account as it works with a support system with organized backend tickets. If you are encountering problems that need support within a project, this tool can help you with it. Free plans are available indefinitely for one account.

TrackDuck – With the use of this powerful tool, you can set up a tiny box in one corner of your site where visitors may send feedback about the interface or bugs and any other issues they want to call your attention on.

Trackduck can easily integrate with other applications like Basecamp for tracking user feedback. A free edition of this app is available to provide all the basic services for one account. If you are just starting and want to test the waters, then this is a great tool for you.

CHAPTER 9: Tips to Improve Sales Performance

There's ample room for improvement on the internet and you will never know what works best until you test it. Meaning, the only way to discover what works well on your website is through constant testing and the best way to start increasing your sales. Here are some tests you can take and see what effects they can have on your business.

#1 - Offer Just one Product or Service on your Home Page

Are you selling multi-products on your websites? If you are and you're still not doing better, try selling just one product or service with more content describing the product and how it can be of use to the user. This way, you are educating the viewers. Giving more information about one product rather than providing them with more products and less information is not beneficial to them. That's why they don't stay much longer to click of the product you are offering on your website.

One way to see if this strategy works is to run the test for a week or two, then see if your sales increased.

#2 - Reposition you Opt-in Offers for List Building

Opt-in offers are usually used to build your list. Through your list, you will be able to connect with your subscribers regularly especially when you offer or launch a new product. Through your list, you are building a set of loyal customers. However, you need to know which part of your web page create the most impact on your customers and visitors.

If you don't have a rather lengthy sales letter, test by placing your opt-in offer on the top left of the page which the most prominent and mostly draws your viewer's eyes first. Or, you can also test placing your opt-in on the top fold of your home page. This is the area of the screen visible to a visitor before they scroll down the page.

If you are using a long letter for your opt-in offer, test by placing it on the second page or after you have grabbed your visitor's attention, establish your credibility by citing years of experience and encouraging testimonials from satisfied customers.

You can also test place your opt-in offer on every page of your site, so it's always in front of your visitors. The more sign–up opportunities you have, the more subscribers can get into your list.

#3 – Promote with Hover Ads

Are you familiar with hover ads? If you aren't, then maybe you are familiar with those small windows that suddenly pop-up once you visit a website. They contain special offers of information. Opt-ups have been useful to marketers before they were blocked by search engines. With this blocking software, visitors had missed a lot of information about some product which could have benefited them.

In lieu of pop-ups, hover ads replaced these pop-ups that behave like pop-ups but they are not real pop-ups so they were not blocked from the system. Test them on your website and you will see how. You can use these hover ads for special offers and see how much percentage of your sales had gone up.

#4 – Feature Product Benefits in your Headline

Headline usually creates an impact on your sales. It's because it's the first thing that visitors set their eyes into once they take a visit to your site. It catches a visitor's attention and compels him to read your sales letter.

#5 - Add Credibility to Enhance Visitor's Trust

Your sales copy must establish your credibility. One way to do this is to include customer testimonials. Make sure they come from genuine expressions of satisfied customers. It is more effective if the testimony elaborates on how the product or service had benefited the customer. This enhances your credibility more if it carries your experience and background. You must aim to convince the viewer or reader that you're the best person they can run to give the specific problems that need to be solved.

#6 – Focus on your Visitors

The most effective sales copy focuses on the viewer and not on you. Too often, the one writing the sales letter uses "I", "me" and "we" instead of "you" and "your."

CHAPTER 10: Elements of a Successful Business

There are 5 important key elements in online business that you need to focus on.

Choosing the Right Niche Market

Choosing the right niche is important in putting up your Internet Business. You can do some research on what most people want. You can also make a survey on your networks to determine their preferences. Study more about your competitors. Others even spied on their competitors' keywords just to be able to grab their page rank.

Currently, most people are interested in health, career, finance, success and business. By knowing what's trending in your network or knowing information related to your communities including their gender, age, locations, etc., you will be able to choose the best niche that will cater to their needs and wants.

Create a Professional Website

After determining your niche and identifying the types of people that are potential customers for your business, create a professional website by following instruction in Chapter 4. Remember how important it is to have a perfect workplace where you can connect with your market.

Offer Products or Services

After creating a great website or domain, make sure that you offer relevant products and service of high quality and value. Performance and quality count much in generating new visitors while retaining loyal customers. Enhancing your customer base depends on how you manage your online business.

Generate More Conversion

Visitors are important to your website but conversion is what makes your business successful. There are websites that generate a lot of traffic but fewer sales conversions. It is essential that you focus your marketing efforts on more targeted traffic that generate buyers and improve your sales. Improve your ads, keywords, offers, etc. Good sales copy to convert many of your visitors into paying customers.

Create System with Technology

If you lack the skill needs in doing some specific task while running your business like putting up your domain or writing relevant and exciting content, you can always outsource them. There are lots of freelancers out there who offer services like writing, designing or SEO services.

After establishing your business, you can improve your website by running it on automation or introduce affiliate marketing. If you don't have enough time to maintain your workplace, you can now have virtual assistant apps that will do administrative tasks for you.

One thing that you should not fail to have is an autoresponder that will send emails, answer queries and build your list automatically. Everything will just be connected to your email address. Auto responders like Aweber, Mailchimps, are just some that will benefit your business most.

Conclusion

Online business can be hard but not impossible. One can reach success through learning by personal observation, and from others who had been ahead in this journey. Like any other business, managing an online business is challenging and sometimes discouraging, but it will instill in you're a kind of character that only those who are diligent learners is worthy of.

Now that you have taken a little knowledge out of this eBook, we wish you would not fail to apply it in your own business until you attain real success. The more that you read, the more you will learn.

However, don't waste your time procrastinating, grabbing everything and losing your focus on what you have been trying to achieve...your GOAL!

Now that we have reached the end of this book, we leave everything you. It's time that you take a step forward regardless where you are at the moment – whether you're just starting or you had started!

****

The End

Passive Income Blueprint:

Your Roadmap To Financial Freedom

Table of Contents

Contents

Introduction

The idea of earning passive income has been around for ages. You surely have folks or relatives earning a decent amount of money from their real estate properties. That's exactly the time-tested way of earning a passive income. But as times are changing, people discover that earning a steady passive income is not limited to rental properties or business activities that do not require material participation, as per the Internal Revenue Service's definition.

With a lot of money-making opportunities out there, it's impossible not to find an opportunity that will allow you to earn passive income nowadays. The best way to learn how to launch and grow a passive income stream is to find out how the successful ones do it. In this book, we compiled the secrets of the top passive income earners. How did they begin it? What are their strategies to keep the business going?

You surely have heard some of the new passive income streams, like investing in dividend stocks and peer to peer lending. My goal is to supplement what you already know by providing you the best practices to these fields. That way, you can start your journey of having a reliable, long-term source of passive income. Who does not want financial freedom and live the life they always wanted? I am here to help you get started your journey to financial freedom, with the help of passive income streams.

Chapter 1: What is Passive Income?

Passive Income is defined as the income obtained with little time and effort needed to maintain it. It is a regular income coming from another source other than a contractor or an employer. According to the American Internal Revenue Service, it is one of the three broad types of income. The other two are active income and portfolio income. Active income is acquired through services performed like compensation or salary. Portfolio income is obtained through dividends, investments, royalties, capital gains, and interest. Passive income is sometimes drawing similarities to portfolio income because it can be in the form of an interest from a bank account; royalties from music, computer software, or books; stock dividends; Internet ads on websites; and pensions.

The IRS limits passive income to rental properties and trade or business that does not require people to materially participate. Once you engage in a trade or business activity for more than 500 hours, it is "material participation." The IRS will not consider you as a passive income earner if you are involved in a business for more than an hour the entire taxable year.

There are financial and government institutions that do not agree with IRS' definition of passive income. Like I mentioned earlier, there are so many passive income sources out there waiting for you to explore and the first on the list is in the succeeding chapter. I like how these ideas make it easy to start a business with little to no capital at all.

Is passive income taxable? The good news is that the tax rates of passive income are lower than that of active income. As per the federal government's ruling, an active income or those derived from wages and salaries fall at 35 percent while passive income is at 15 percent. While it makes sense that earning passive income requires little effort to keep it going, you will actually need to exert time, hard work, and effort if you want to build real wealth out of it. Truth is, creating passive income is not a passive activity. Do note that some activities are just more passive than others. Contrary to popular belief, earning a passive income is not a get rich quick scheme or as laidback as sitting in a coffee shop while you enjoy sipping your favorite Frappuccino. It requires lots of work, time, and even resources for it to succeed.

Does it mean that you have to go to a complicated process before you can earn a steady passive income? It can be laborious in the beginning, yes, especially when you are just getting started. But once you get the hang of it, you will discover that there are ways to make it a little less complicated. How? Automate and outsource. These are two of the best ways to keep your business running. As the name suggests, outsourcing refers to a good or service obtained from an outside supplier. You might have come across websites that allow you to outsource workers. Automating work, on the other hand, requires applications and services to get started.

Chapter 2: Are passive income really achievable?

The answer is yes! Because it exists for quite some time now, the idea of earning passive income is not questionable. Many people around the globe are enjoying their steady flow of passive income. I, myself, have friends who earn cash while they sleep. The real question here is how you can make it happen in your own life. In this chapter, I will share with you how successful passive income earners get to the top of their game. These are four strategies real passive income earners do.

Visualizing success

Successful passive income earners imagine success and work for it. Pat Flynn, a passive income whiz who founded SmartPassiveIncome.com believes success is not accidental. He believes people should have at least one adage that would reflect people and his is "the harder you work, the luckier you become." Think of the law of attraction. When you think of success as something not bound to happen, you will eventually shudder at working a little harder. But if you believe that success is for you, the universe will help you get through it. Luck, in the end, is not by chance but the choices we make.

Understanding your niche

These people don't serve just anybody or everybody. Anyone running a successful business knows the importance of understanding a good niche. It's all about being clear about what you want to offer. What are these products and services? Who is your target market? For example, you want to launch a new website about fashion and makeup. Your target market would be young girls who have the purchasing power. So basically, you focus on fashion and makeup. After understanding a good niche, it's time to identify the needs of your customers.

Evaluating people's needs and wants

Successful passive income earners focus on their customer's needs. Later in this book, I will give you more insights about creating digital products and how you can earn passive income from them. Let's say you are planning to write an eBook. Perhaps you already have your business plan and you have an idea what you would include on your eBook chapters. But have you asked your ideal readers what they actually want or need? It takes some courage to ask and if you're not yet ready for something like this, it is fine to join Facebook groups and see what your ideal clients are talking about. I join several Facebook groups on my niche. I participate in the discussions.

Creating a logical plan

Let's say you are planning to open an online shop and sell items from home. You cannot decide whether you will create your own product or source from a manufacturer. Creating your own product works when you already master it and it will not be time-consuming. Examples are digital products like eBooks.

You learned that sourcing product is more convenient and time-saving. So you contacted manufacturers. They helped you have the products you need for your online shop. Later on, you learned that the manufacturer is willing to send those orders directly to your buyers. All you needed to do is get their information. That refers to drop shipping and that will be tackled in one chapter of this book.

I mentioned drop shipping because I wanted to emphasize how hard it is to make choices in launching a new venture. This is where planning comes into the picture. I recommend that you have a business plan before you begin. I heard so many stories of people failing with their startups not because the business was not profitable enough but because they did not have the right strategy. They suffer from information overload. A business plan can help you organize your thoughts and be clear about your goals.

A business plan that works has a heart-centered approach. What does it mean? Michael E. Gerber, a New York Times best-selling author and entrepreneur, described it as an approach that starts with experiencing the feelings you have. This is far cry from the traditional business plan that is normally head-centric, meaning it begins with logics, thoughts, and reasons.

Chapter 3: Dividend's stock investment

The steady payments are the number one reason why many people put money into dividend-paying stocks. What are dividend stocks, if you may ask? The dividend is the payment made by a corporation to its shareholders. However, companies do not always distribute payouts in cash. There are times when they distribute additional stocks to their shareholders and this is what we meant by stock dividends. The returns in dividend investing are usually small but you can increase the value by selling stocks.

Want to invest in dividend stocks? As a beginner, invest in low volatility stocks first. Just because a stock is high-yielding means it will produce a high total return. Those who wish to create a stable growing dividend income should reconsider about taking big risks at the very start. There are reasons why there are high dividend stocks and one of this is an underlying business problem.

If that is the case then how are you going to choose the best dividend stocks? Many investors would agree that the secret lies in the long-term success of a company. Here are questions you might want to research when choosing a dividend investing strategy:

- What is the financial health of the company?
- Does the company have the ability to increase its payout over time?
- How does the management treat their investors?
- Does the company have an excellent credit rating?

Dividend investing is ideal for people with long-term prospects. How long should it be? Warren Buffett, one of the most successful investors in the world, believes the best holding period for stocks is "forever."

I mentioned management in the questions above. I want to emphasize the importance of researching their historical treatment of dividends. Did the company face a difficult financial time? How did the management handle it? You will realize that there are more questions you will ask in the long run because the management has a huge impact on the financial health of a company. I agree with Buffett's belief that a stock should be kept as long as possible.

Chapter 4: Rental properties

Owning a rental property can be both a blessing and a curse. It's no secret that there are tenants from hell or those who demand a lot and pay late. But let's focus on the powerful, beautiful side of having a real estate property of your own. Rental properties are one of the earliest known sources of passive income. Nowadays, people would rather rent spaces than deal with the increasing rate of property tax and if you already have a property, you can use it as an asset. As an owner of a rental property, take into considerations these important factors to guarantee passive income in the long run.

Rental property maintenance

Basically, it's unfair to set a high rental rate when the property is in bad shape. Maintenance works are one of the dreaded tasks of homeowners. But if you're planning to rent it out, this is really something you need to do unless you decided to rent it out at a cheap price. Before charging more for rent, make sure that the house is well-maintained. Do some repaint, refinish the inside, or do some landscaping to the yard.

New Ways to Create listings

Airbnb is a marketplace where travelers can list, discover, and book unique accommodations around the world. You can be a host and rent out your extra space by signing up to marketplaces like Airbnb. A list serves as a profile page of your place. Airbnb is a good place to start hosting your property.

Finding the right neighborhood

If you are still planning to buy a property for rental purposes, spend a lot of time finding the right one. Joseph Hogue, an investment analyst, believes it is a huge mistake to buy and rent out a property in a lower-income neighborhood. Some people think they will eventually get a huge discount when they buy a property that costs half less than better areas. Unpaid rent and repairs alone can be the two factors why it's not ideal to buy a property in the low-income neighborhood and have it rented out.

Putting your rentals in Limited Liability Companies (LLC)

LLCs protect investors from liability on rental properties. The risk is always part of owning a rental property and whether you like it or not, that property is vulnerable to potential lawsuits. Your assets will eventually be affected when the property is under your name. When thinking of putting your property in LLC, research its pros and cons first. Ask a legal expert and determine whether an LLC is for you.

Owning a rental property can be a rewarding experience. It will surely give you steady passive income just as long as you have the right strategy.

Chapter 5: Peer to Peer Lending Platform

Peer to Peer lending or crowdlending is the practice of lending money to individuals or businesses through online services that match lenders directly with borrowers. Here's an example of how it works: You wanted to open a small gift shop and you need around $30,000 for the startup. Because you have insufficient funds to cover all the startup expenses, you went to a bank to apply for a loan. You presented your business model. However, the bank was not impressed with your idea and rejected your proposal.

While looking for an alternative, you stumbled upon a crowdlending website. The website allowed you to borrow the capital you need. Investor A lends you $25, Investor B lends $100, and so on until you reached $30,000. The crowdlending website split the investment across a range of borrowers to reduce the risk. This is called Notes.

These lenders earn cash thru interest. If you are interested in starting a P2P business, automated investing sites are the best way to go. P2P is a rising business these days because P2P online platforms make it more convenient to borrow money. Banks are stricter when it comes to checking credentials. Applying for a bank loan can take up to three months while borrowing thru P2P can take approximately 12 days.

Online credit marketplace like Prosper.com and Lending Club evaluates the client information for you. These platforms will match you directly on borrowers based on certain criteria. All you have to do is select loans in which to invest.

How much can you earn through P2P lending? Returns vary depending on the platform. These automated investing sites will calculate how much you could earn on a Note. The more notes that you invest in, the higher the returns. There are various factors that influence returns.

What is the risk in P2P? Any loan has risks involved. There is no security in P2P. You will lose money when the borrowers failed to pay. The good thing about joining an online credit marketplace is that they could help you collect payments in case the borrower missed a payment. How will you lower the potential for losses? Spread out your investment through a variety of borrowers.

While there are risks involved, P2P lending can be a win-win situation for both lenders and borrowers when done right. Borrowers can apply without a hassle. Those who borrowed to launch their business can repay the loan while growing their ventures. Lenders can choose who to lend to while enjoying a steady stream of passive income.

Chapter 6: EBook Publishing Business

The publishing world is changing really fast. Gone were the days when people have to go through a scrutiny of a publishing company before seeing their book printed. Nowadays, you can sell your book without too much hassle and earn royalties from it. More and more people are taking advantage of self-publishing. Living in a fast-paced world can be a good thing, too. Almost all people choose to read straight from their smartphones and tablets and this can be a money-making opportunity. Even those newspaper and magazine publishers are relying on digital subscriptions from their readers.

Start as an infopreneur. What is an infopreneur? Tim Ferriss' "The Four Hour Work Week" is one of the best-selling books about passive income. If you already read the book, you surely know that Ferriss wants you to kill the nine to five and escape the office. But it was also noticeable that in the book, Ferriss stressed two things: the importance of information products and selecting a niche you know. By information products, Ferriss means eBooks, blogs, and podcasts or anything that enlightens people.

You can start your journey as an "infopreneur" by self publishing or create a digital product like an eBook. How much can you earn by writing e-Books? This is perhaps the biggest question you have in mind right now. Your possible earnings vary from platform to platform. You can sell the book from $.99 up to $19. You can also sell it on your own website. Apparently, the price should depend on the quality and quantity of a book. Before self-publishing, your book, take note of these five important considerations.

Conduct a market research.

Sadly, this is one of the important factors that some authors ignore. If you want to write an eBook that sells, it matters to conduct your research. It is not hard as it looks like. Start your own group of friends. Interview these people. Are they concerned most about their dating life? Write about tips on maintaining relationships. Are they asking you advice about handling finances? Write about wealth. Other than wealth and relationship topics, health and personal passions are the other niches that sell.

Provide value.

You might be tempted to start with a self-help book because self-improvement is such a big business. Do note that not all self-help books work. A self-help book should be backed by science for it to be effective. Providing value can also be done by focusing on "how to." The number of topics is endless and you are more on the safe side. How-to topics work because it creates curiosity.

Familiarize yourself with proper formatting.

Digital platforms like Amazon's Kindle and Barnes and Noble's Nook have strict standards when it comes to formatting eBooks. Save it to PDF before sending it to the publishers who could help you convert it into epub format. Aside from following the correct format, it's also a must to have an attractive cover. It's important that you have the relevant images to attract readers. You may want to hire a freelancer who could help you design your eBook cover. Believe me, there are simplistic eBooks that made it simply because of the eBook design. It's normal for people to judge based on appearance. So exert a bit more on the cover or get help from experts.

Think outside the box

If you want to create fiction books such as science fiction, fantasy, and romance, be extra-creative. Read books and watch movies in your favorite genre. Go out, walk, and talk to people. I do these when I am out of inspiration to write. There are so many things you can do to unleash creativity. Sometimes, the creative juice is flowing at the least expected time so I suggest that you keep a notepad and a pen in handy just in case. I have to say that fiction books are more complicated to write unless of course, you really have the talent in writing.

Chapter 7: YouTube channel

For you to earn money from your videos, you will need to join the YouTube Partner Program. From there, set up your AdSense account. It's actually easier to apply for an AdSense account for YouTube than for a blog or website. Just make sure that your account is enabled for monetization. Once you become a "host account" or your account has been approved for AdSense and you get hits, expect to receive your payment once it exceeded $100. You can also choose which videos you want to monetize.

YouTube determines your earnings depending on the type of ads and their pricing. Take note that there are types of videos that are not eligible. AdSense is strict when it comes to commercial rights, so try to make everything as original as possible. If, in case, you really need to use a certain music as background, provide a proper attribution. Also take note that monetization is currently not available to all countries. You may want to check first if your country is allowed to have it. Check their copyright and community guidelines.

Now there are only two things you need to ask yourself before monetizing your YouTube channel. First, do you have an audience? Second, can you create engaging videos on a regular basis? If the answer to these questions is yes, it's time for you to get started but let's discuss these two factors first.

Audience before the income. This is a golden rule if you want to start earning a passive income from your YouTube channel. Growing your audience requires learning about Search Engine Optimization or SEO. For a video to be discovered, it should have searchable titles. Let's say you have a baking channel. If I were the one searching for a certain no-bake recipe, I would rather click a headline that says "Easy 3-Ingredient No-Bake Dessert" than the one that says "No-bake peanut butter dessert." The secret in creating a catchy title is to be creative while keeping the necessary keywords on your title.

The last and perhaps, the more important thing to consider, is your capability to produce YouTube videos on a regular basis. Once you have an audience or subscribers, these people will surely wait for your next video. Invest in a good camera and learn about video editing software. It matters to have good audio as well, so you might want to invest in a decent mic.

Chapter 8: Online Coaching Business

Interactions and connections are the two most important factors to keep in mind when starting an online coaching business. Basically, you don't want people to think that you're there just because you want their money. People will not trust you unless they know you and they like you.

Having a real-life accomplishment on a certain niche is one big advantage in starting an online coaching business. For example, you've been training people to be fit for years now. Use your previous experience to be an online fitness coach. Establish yourself as an expert. How will you do this? Start by focusing on a niche service. When you coach a niche you are passionate about, it's given that you will attract the right clients.

Judy Jablon, an early childhood consultant says there are three steps in powerful interaction. The first is being present which means you say and do things with effectiveness and maximum clarity. The second one is a connection. You should have a deeper relationship with the person you're coaching. The third and most important step is extend learning. Have you thought the person the best practices to attach to those learnings?

Now your goal is to let people know about you. How to get other people know you before presenting your services? Show your face or do a Facebook Live coaching. Have a well-written "About Me" page. Share your stories. Making people like you is another story. I know one strategy that works. Be relatable. Notice how we like people who have something in common with us? Like, someone who has the same name as us. People tend to be more comfortable with what they know because an "unfamiliar territory" is basically hard to trust. Being liked is one way to influence people. Once you get people like you, building trust is not that hard to achieve at all.

As a coach, your audience expects a lot from you like you are the type of person who makes the best decisions in life. If you, yourself is facing some life issues and you don't have any help, you won't likely meet that expectation. Remember, how you are and what you say will affect how others think about you. You can grow your coaching business through social media and blogging. Create helpful and inspiring content on a regular basis.

Chapter 9: Affiliate Marketing

Affiliate marketing is endorsing other people's products and services and getting a compensation after successfully referring others. Aside from receiving a percentage of the sale, it's also possible to get a fixed amount per every lead. A lead does not necessarily purchase but uses your affiliate link to sign up. Most affiliate programs will require you to have a blog or a website. There are also some that only require a social page. Below are 10 of the best affiliate programs that you may use whether you are a newbie or an experienced blogger.

1. Amazon- as their associate, Amazon will give you the access to their programs and earn up to 6% on local referrals. They also offer up to 75% discounts on products and local services.
2. SiteGround- it is by far one of the best hosting companies these days. For every referral, they will pay you $65.
3. Shareasale- what I like most about this affiliate network is that they will pay you for every lead and every sale. They offer $1 per lead and a generous $100 per sale. I recommend this to publishers looking for a decent pay-per-lead program.
4. eBay- their in-house affiliate program gives as much as 200% referral bonus for new or reactivated buyers. Once accepted, you will have access to eBay's Publisher Portal where you could get banners, text links, and buttons. You can use these on your websites and even social pages.
5. Rakuten Linkshare- dubbed as the global leader in performance marketing, they require you have a loyal following on your website before you can sign up. Work on your blog and strive to get as many hits as possible.
6. Viglink- as a publisher, you will get a snippet code that will automatically turn existing links on your page into revenue generating links. You will earn a commission once a user makes a purchase.
7. Ideal Shape- this weight loss website will pay you $10 for every blog post you write about their products or website.
8. Clickbank- you will be given a unique link that you can use to promote products. They will give you a free book that you can use as a guide.
9. FlexOffers- they have thousands of products- right from clothing and accessories down to online and legal services that you can promote on your website. Once you become a publisher, you can also earn money by referring new publishers to their network.
10. AWeber- it is free to join in this email marketing program. You could earn up to 30% lifetime recurring commission per referral. They pay through Check.

Affiliate marketing is not limited to cash. Some merchants render huge discounts as compensation for every customer you bring in. This is also called a referral program. Take note that referral program and affiliate marketing program also have few differences. In referral program, the goal is to promote something to make people's lives better while in affiliate marketing, your goal is to earn a living for yourself. Some companies provide discounts when you sign up or refer customers. These are some of the merchants that offer rewards other than cash. While these will not give you passive income, you can take advantage of the rewards to save some cash.

1. Dropbox- this file hosting service lets you store all your photos, videos, and files in one place. You can also access them anywhere. When you have a free account, you only have around 2GB of space. You could earn extra space by referring your friends. You could earn 500 MB per referral when you have a free account and 1 GB per referral when you have a pro account.
2. Evernote- this freemium app is designed for note taking and organizing. You will earn 5 points for every friend you refer. You can use the points to get their Premium account.
3. CriCut- there are affiliates that won't require you to promote. Simply sign up to their program and you will already get a discount. CriCut, an electronic cutting machine brand, offers up to 30% discount to their affiliates.
4. Montage- you will get a free photo book once your review is approved. At least that's something you can keep for a lifetime!
5. Freebie Direct- they will help you offer free stuff to entice site visitors and increase your readership. This can work for both new and mid-level website owners.

When promoting your affiliate programs, never sound like you are advertising it. Create an epic post and mention a certain product. There are creative ways to do it. One effective way to do it is to create an honest review of a certain product. You can do it through a video or through your blog. A product tutorial post will be of great help to readers. Or better, do a mini giveaway.

As a publisher, giving away a freebie will also benefit you because you could build trust. You can also grow your followers by offering the freebie in exchange for their follows and likes. You can also include affiliate links on the giveaway page.

Chapter 10: Drop ship

A drop shipping business is a supply chain management method wherein you don't have to keep goods in stock. Instead, you transfer a customer's shipment details and orders to another retailer or a manufacturer. Drop shipping can be a good source of passive income because it's pretty easy to maintain. But like any business model, it has both pros and cons too.

For now, I want you to focus on the good side of drop shipping. What I like most about drop shipping is that you can do it from home. There is no need to bother about keeping an inventory of stocks and since you don't need to set up a physical store, you have the freedom to offer more items to your buyers. Isn't it more convenient when you don't have to take care of everything? Eventually, someone else is responsible for customer care and shipping the items to the buyer.

You may want to start on Fulfillment by Amazon (FBA). When you already have a "Selling on Amazon" account, simply add FBA and start creating your product listings. Once a customer orders a product, Amazon will be the one picking, packing, and shipping the item. That sounds easy but read all their guidelines to make sure you're doing it right.

On eBay, it is called product sourcing. As a seller, you are not obliged to handle an item. All you have to do is collect the money from the buyer and forward it to a product source. Like the FBA, the product source on eBay will be responsible for sending the item straight to the buyer.

As someone who does business, it matters to find the best partners. This is actually the most challenging part of running a drop shipping business. If the manufacturer, unfortunately, ships the wrong items or if there is a long delay, you will eventually piss off your customers.

You can abstain from such blunder by researching carefully your drop shipping partners. A trustworthy drop shipping supplier does not ask for membership fees or pre-order fees. Genuine suppliers are willing to accept orders via email and they consist of expert staff. Sometimes, it's not enough that you search on Google. Be careful because there are a lot of spammy listings out there. The best way to find a drop shipping wholesaler is to contact the manufacturer directly.

There are a few techniques to have a successful drop shipping business. One strategy is to focus on niche merchandise. It's quite hard to serve everybody. Focus on the group of people who will likely buy your products. Because you provide specific services, there will be less competition so you don't have to bother about marketing too much.

Chapter 11: App Development

You don't need to be a rocket scientist to develop an app. With patience, time, and enthusiasm, I believe there is no reason for you not to learn it. You can even do it right from home without any background in programming. Sounds cool. But, how?

Write down whatever idea you have in mind and create a mockup of that idea using a prototyping tool. As a beginner, it's a must to start with a prototype. A prototyping tool is usually offered for free and will let you test your app without writing any code. You can also use this tool to get feedback from potential customers. Testing the water before releasing a full version an app will save you from potential flops. Some of the well-known prototype websites for apps are Marvel App, InVision, and Fluidui.com.

If you're interested in creating iOS apps for iPhone and iPad, you have to learn about Apple's Swift. This programming language begins with a lesson that enables you to build a simple app. You will get an idea how the code and interface look like at the end of the lesson. For you to create an app using Switch, it's required that you use a Mac computer running the latest version of Xcode. Simply create an Apple ID and download the Xcode for free from the App Store.

Aside from reading Apple's documentation on their programming language, I suggest that you take advantage of free courses and step-by-step tutorials offered by developers. People have different learning styles. Some of us learn better by reading while some by watching videos.

What's next after building an app? It's time to submit it to the App Store. It should be easy since it's the developer's task to upload the app on their website. All you need to do is sign up to the app store and pay the membership fee. The fees vary depending on the app store. Apple requires an annual fee of $99 for individuals and $299 for their enterprise program or those who create organization-exclusive applications. Google only requires a one-time fee of $25 using Google Payments Merchant account. Creating Android apps also requires installing an app called Android Studio. As a beginner, I recommend you join Google's free course on Android development.

Chapter 12: Hobbies

Do you love taking pictures? Then take this hobby as a money-making activity! Yes, you can make money out of your passion for photography. One simple way to do this is to create stock photography.

What is stock photography? It's a supply of pictures that is often licensed for commercial design purposes. Stock photos are usually accessed via online databases and can be bought at a low cost. These databases are like the "supermarket" of photos. With thousands of images at these photo libraries, how will you make your pictures stand out?

Before selling your photos to those websites, make sure that you checked their guidelines first. This is especially important if you are new to this field. It will give you an idea what kind of photos to submit and the subjects these sites are actually looking for.

Speaking of subjects, one study noted that people are attracted to photos showing other people than those that only show abstract or nature. Do note, however, that showing emotion is one of the reasons why these kinds of photo sell. Think of dramatic effects or dynamics. This can be done by mastering the rule of thirds.

In photography terms, this is simplified as the "focal point of a person." The rule of thirds technique is done by putting the main subject either on the left or the right but never in the direct middle of a photo. The alignment produces a sense of direction. This is ideal if you want to create more emotion and dynamics on your photos.

Meanwhile, what if you want to focus on a certain niche? There is nothing bad about it as long as that niche aligns with your passion. For example, you want to pay particular attention to wedding photography. Make sure that you have all the right equipment, like a high-quality DSLR camera, lenses, lens filters, diffuser and reflector kit. Take note that tools differ depending on your niche. The tool needed for food photography can be different from that of wedding photography. It's also a must that you are familiar with photo editing software.

If you are planning to sell your photos, you can start with the help of stock photography agencies. Examples are Evanto Market, Shutterstock, and Fotolia. These agencies buy stock photos. You can earn passive income from the royalties you will get per image. Some agencies even offer referral programs that you could also take advantage of.

Conclusion

If you have decided what type of passive income stream you would like to set up, I would like to congratulate you for it. Stick to those ideas. Who knows, that could be a million dollar idea. That said, all you need to do is an act. Do some action plan and if it fails, don't give up. There are other sources of passive income waiting for you to try. If you still haven't, I hope you could use this book as a reference once day.

I love hearing stories of people earning some pretty good cash while they sleep. They have the freedom to travel the world and spend more time with their loved ones. That is the essence of being financially independent. I hope to hear your story of success one day.

Lastly, thank you for reading this book!

****

The End

www.ingramcontent.com/pod-product-compliance
Lightning Source LLC
Chambersburg PA
CBHW081844170526

45167CB00007B/2902